W9-BSN-509

NEWTON COUNTY PUBLIC LIBRARY
ROSELAWN BRANCH

Unsolved Extraterrestrial Mysteries

NEWTON COUNTY PUBLIC LIBRARY
ROSELAWN BRANCH

Mysteries and Conspiracies™

Unsolved Extraterrestrial Mysteries

David Southwell and Sean Twist

ROSEN PUBLISHING®

New York

NEWTON COUNTY PUBLIC LIBRARY
ROSELAWN BRANCH

North American edition first published in 2008 by:

The Rosen Publishing Group, Inc.
29 E. 21st Street
New York, NY 10010

North American edition copyright © 2008 by The Rosen Publishing Group, Inc. First published as *Conspiracy Theories* in Australia, copyright © 2004 by Carlton Books Limited. Text copyright © 2004 by David Southwell. Additional end matter copyright © The Rosen Publishing Group, Inc.

North American edition book design: Tahara Anderson

All rights reserved. No part of this book may be reproduced in any form without permission in writing from the publisher, except by a reviewer.

Library of Congress Cataloging-in-Publication Data

Southwell, David.
Unsolved extraterrestrial mysteries / David Southwell and Sean Twist.
    p.cm. — (Mysteries and conspiracies)
Includes bibliographical references and index.
ISBN-13: 978-1-4042-1080-6
ISBN-10: 1-4042-1080-6
1. Human-alien encounters. 2. Alien abduction. 3. Unidentified flying objects.
I. Twist, Sean. II. Title.
BF2050.S62 2007
001.942–dc22

                                                                2007004169

Manufactured in the United States of America

On the cover: *(Left)* A B-2 stealth bomber refuels in midair; *(right)* artist's rendition of the aliens known as the Greys.

CONTENTS

1 ALIEN ABDUCTIONS

One of the most prevalent conspiracy theories disturbing the sleep of millions today is that of alien abductions. All over the world, the lives of innocent men and women are apparently being disrupted by incidents of otherworldly kidnappings. Suddenly, they find themselves forcibly removed from their homes, transported to alien crafts or environments where they are horribly violated by creatures from beyond the stars. What makes these incidents all the more terrifying is the complete helplessness of the victims, who are at the mercy of these inscrutable aliens and their disturbing medical procedures.

Researchers of alien abductions have attempted to categorize the kidnappings, searching for common threads of experience among abductees. Among those categories is the basic physical abduction, where abductees talk of

The Greys — the aliens most commonly alleged to abduct humans

feeling tranquilized, then watching placidly as they are moved to an alien ship. They might be moved there by a smaller craft, by some form of tractor beam, or by some kind of interdimensional "gate." Some abductees report being moved directly through solid objects, such as the walls of a house.

Another popular form is the bio-energy extraction method: the abductees' bio-energy, or consciousness, is removed from their bodies by an alien technology that usually takes the form of a white to bluish-white beam of light surrounding and penetrating their bodies. The victims' consciousness is often inserted into another body before being returned to its original form.

There are also the telepathic lucid dream versions of abductions, which, while not being as physical in nature as a corporeal abduction, are no less damaging. In this kind of attack, abductees find themselves experiencing a lucid dream created by aliens, in which a normal dream disintegrates and is replaced by telepathic messages or visual images. As in the bio-extraction scenario, a beam of whitish energy emanating from the ceiling above them is sometimes seen by awakening victims.

While abductions have been reported throughout history, there seems to be an increase in frequency of late. It's almost as if the perpetrators—aliens, or whoever is responsible for these heinous crimes against humanity—are growing increasingly desperate.

THE STRANGE PART

Throughout the ages, abduction has been one of the great themes of horror stories. Some even try to suggest that links between abduction by fairies and abduction by little grey men makes them one and the same. Maybe they are, but only in the sense that our collective minds updated our nightmares after watching Steven Spielberg's *Close Encounters of the Third Kind*.

THE USUAL SUSPECTS

The Greys

The Greys are the most common type of alien experienced in the abduction scenario. Small creatures with melon-shaped heads and huge, black, slanted eyes, they are at the root of many alien conspiracy theories. The current thoughts on their involvement in abductions are varied, from an optimistic hope that they are our descendants coming back in time to save the earth from destruction, to a darker suspicion that they are extracting sperm and ova from humans to save their own race. Under this hypothesis, the Greys are a race of clones that has lost the ability to reproduce sexually; the Greys hope to create a hybrid between themselves and humans in order to survive.

The U.S. Government

The Majestic 12—also known as MJ-12—is a powerful shadow group within the U.S. government that may be working with the Greys, allowing them to continue their experiments in exchange for technology. This deal has allegedly helped give rise to weapons such as the B-2 stealth bomber and the F-117 stealth fighter. Many abductees recall seeing military personnel and installations, often without seeing aliens. (This poses the question of whether this arrangement is merely a matter of working in conjunction with the Greys, or whether the U.S government has its own agenda—perhaps mind control?) Using masterful disinformation tactics, this group discredits and ridicules any research into UFOs and indeed, anything else that may shed light on the mysterious Greys, thereby ensuring continued abduction work, continued misery for thousands, and continued technological payoffs for the U.S. government.

THE UNUSUAL SUSPECTS

Dolphins

The Greys may be either future descendants of dolphins or genetic extrapolations of dolphins that travel back to our time for their own nefarious purposes. The similarities between Greys and dolphins, in skin texture, color, and their ability to emanate an ultrasonic blast to stun enemies (Greys use "the stare" to subdue abductees, for example), bear consideration.

MOST CONVINCING EVIDENCE

Following abduction experiences, many victims have found themselves implanted with small metal devices, usually in the nasal cavities, but often in other areas of the body. When these implants are successfully removed by surgeons, their origins become no less clear. The metal that is used in many of these devices is unknown to today's science, and their purpose remains an unsettling mystery. Are they tracking devices, or something more?

MOST MYSTERIOUS FACT

The commonality of experience among abduction victims, from descriptions of the Greys, procedures, and implants, is disquieting. The meteoric rise of books, movies, and reports of abductions hints that a greater truth is lurking just beneath the surface, ready to break through at any moment.

SKEPTICALLY SPEAKING

The same phenomenon occurred at the end of the nineteenth century. Although then, instead of alien abductions, it was fairies. Chalk it up to end-of-the-century madness, coupled with premillennial paranoia.

2 CATTLE MUTILATIONS

For decades, cattle farmers around the world have been plagued by a problem, a problem that is as inexplicable as it is horrifying: the grisly puzzle of cattle mutilations. Representing more than just a simple financial loss associated with missing livestock, this exercise in abject cruelty may have a purpose, but like its perpetrators, that purpose remains cloaked in shadows.

While the majority of cattle mutilation cases occur in the United States (particularly in New Mexico), the phenomenon has been reported in Puerto Rico, South America, and Canada. Details of the mutilations may vary from case to case, but there are enough commonalities to suggest an orchestrated program of sorts is underway. More often that not, the bodies of mutilated animals are found drained of blood. Missing organs have been removed with surgical precision, with the carcass often appearing to have been cauterized. The perpetrators show a particular interest in sensory organs such as the eyes, the reproductive and defecatory systems, and the anterior digestive tract.

As many as 10,000 cattle may have died in this manner, and as a result, several theories have sprung up surrounding this disturbing trend. If dealing with predators, disease, and rowdy young men in search of cow-tipping weren't enough, cattle ranchers now have to contend with an unknown sadistic force that comes and goes like an eviscerating thief in the night.

THE STRANGE PART

Usually, no marks are found around the bodies of the mutilated cattle, with the exception of a few tripod marks surrounding the bodies. Clamp marks have been found on some cattle, suggesting that the mutilation takes place somewhere other than the field in which they are found.

THE USUAL SUSPECTS

UFOs

The theory that aliens (such as the Greys) are seeking to find a way to save their race through bonding with our own gene pool strays into the arena of cattle mutilation. The aliens could somehow be using cow blood and organs in their experiments, possibly because bovine parts are similar

in chemistry to their own. More optimistic theories suggest the aliens are using cows to run random radiation tests in their efforts to save us all from nuclear annihilation. This is backed up by the reports of some human abductees, who claim to have seen cows being led on board UFOs while they themselves were suffering experimentation. UFOs are often seen in the sky in the nights preceding cattle mutilations, and cattle have been known to become restless and stampede when a UFO is visible. This would seem to indicate that cows in general have had more experience with UFOs than they are letting on.

Black Helicopters

Black helicopters have also been seen around cattle fields preceding mutilations, startling cattle with white-hot search-lights. The presence of such mysterious craft would lend credence to the theory that the animals are airlifted away to be mutilated, with their dead bodies simply being dropped back into the field after the process is completed. The black helicopters are often associated with secret government programs and the rise of the New World Order, which could possibly be using cattle to test powerful chemical weapons without hindrance of government guidelines.

(opposite page) The clinical precision and lack of blood renders some cattle mutilations practically inexplicable.

Satanists

First thought to be responsible for the mutilations, satanists were alleged to be using the cows as part of their profane ceremonies, so much so that they were investigated by law enforcement agencies. Nothing conclusive was ever found.

Also suspected: U.S. military; major chemical companies.

THE UNUSUAL SUSPECTS

Natural Predators

Despite the precision of the mutilations and despite the lack of any footprints leading up to the bodies, wolves, coyotes, or so-far-undiscovered predators are thought to be responsible.

El Chupacabra

A mythical monster from Central America, el Chupacabra, referred to as "the Goat Eater," may be responsible for cattle attacks, perhaps in an effort to expand its palate.

Unknown Cattle Disease

An especially virulent, and as yet undiscovered, cattle ailment has also been blamed—a virus so powerful and quick that it can remove the organs and the blood in the space of a single night and then completely vanish from any forensic detection.

MOST CONVINCING EVIDENCE

The neatness of the organ removal, coupled with the complete exsanguination of the bodies, points towards a high degree of technological sophistication, rather than to tooth and claw. Wounds are found to be cauterized, which could be the work of laser cutters. What is interesting is that such technology was not in use when the first cattle mutilations were reported, back in the early 1970s. The blood is also removed with such attention to detail that not one drop can be found around the bodies. This would seem to indicate either military or extraterrestrial involvement, with the parties involved slipping up only occasionally by leaving clamp marks on the animals' legs.

MOST MYSTERIOUS FACT

After the bodies are returned to their fields, they are totally shunned by other animals. There is something so fundamentally wrong with the bodies that even carrion specialists, such as crows, vultures, and the like, will not touch them.

SKEPTICALLY SPEAKING

Why would aliens need cow blood in their efforts to inter-breed with humanity? Wouldn't it make more sense to kidnap gorillas or other members of the ape family? Surely the suspected government collaborators in the Trilateral Commission could get them a few rhesus monkeys from research facilities, no questions asked? Cattle mutilations could be nothing more than a twisted version of the crop circle phenomenon, with well-organized pranksters equipped with medical equipment and vacuum cleaners killing cattle in the dead of night instead of tramping down wheat in circular designs in some poor unsuspecting farmer's field.

3 ALIENS IN HOLLYWOOD

Have extraterrestrial forces taken an active interest in the world's entertainment industry? It would seem reasonable that if the aliens are here and are planning at some point to come out of the closet, then it might be better to soften us up first by preparing us for the idea. The best way to get the idea of outer-space visitors seeded casually into the public consciousness is through the use of television and film, in dramas and documentaries, and the best place to do that from is Hollywood, the heart of the world's film industry.

Over recent years there has been a glut of sci-fi films, television shows, and documentaries dealing with certain common themes. These include "aliens who arrive without warning and try to take over the world," as in *Independence Day, Space: Above And Beyond,* and *V.* These are the ones who appear out of nowhere all over the world and sooner or

Hollywood has recently produced a range of films filled with alien invaders.

later, start killing people, only to be beaten off. Then you get the theme of "opposing aliens using Earth as part of their on-going battle," as in *The X-Files*, with its evil aliens trying to enslave humanity and the rebel aliens who are against this. Finally, there are the "aliens who are our friends next door," like *Men in Black*; *E.T., the Extraterrestrial*; or *Cocoon*, who arrive in limited numbers and prove to be, in general, rather friendly.

The message this is sending is clear: aliens who appear suddenly in massive numbers are evil, whereas the ones who approach subtly, in small numbers or isolated areas, are actually our friends. This is perfect propaganda for the Greys—the small, large-eyed, noseless aliens—who are here in small numbers, carrying out subtle research on us as part of their technology deal with the U.S. government.

Once the public has been prepared sufficiently to be able to cope with the revelation of extraterrestrial contact, the news will be broken over a period of years. The process will start with an official sighting of "something unexplainable," and end with a statement along the lines of "We've found them, here they are." In 1998, a panel of previously skeptical world scientists announced officially that some UFO sightings did provide evidence for aliens on Earth, and NASA astronauts made a sighting of something unexplainable, so it could be that the process has already begun—but is it for the good of humanity?

THE STRANGE PART

It could be that the major theme park and movie companies have a significant part to play in progress of this conspiracy. One of them was rumored to be creating a space exhibit for touring around the United States. This exhibit was to focus on extraterrestrial encounters and generate enormous publicity for the "fact" that Roswell happened and that there was a conspiracy between the U.S. government and the Greys. Some feel that it would have been used to prepare the public for an impending announcement by the government on the reality of UFOs.

THE USUAL SUSPECTS

The Greys

These are the little critters so familiar to popular culture, with the roughly triangular heads, big oval eyes, and little slit mouths. They get their name from the color of their skin. They are here for research purposes and have been in league with the U.S. government ever since the Roswell crash. While the government still believes that they are interested in mutual advancement, they may well be after something far more sinister—such as humans for breeding purposes.

The U.S. Government

Aliens may just be a way of diverting attention from the U.S. government's own experiments into human biology and psychological manipulation. By implanting the myth of the Greys into the public consciousness, state scientists are able to get up to all sorts of unpleasant research without fear of the repercussions. Their ultimate goal is, of course, a weapon that will allow world domination.

THE UNUSUAL SUSPECTS

The Nordics

Another race of aliens, conforming strangely to the old Nazi vision of the Master Race—all, muscular, human-like beings with short blond hair—may be behind the manipulation. The Nordics are aware that the Greys are working with the government for sinister purposes, and they want to help humanity, so they are trying to portray the Greys as sinister. Hollywood is an ideological battlefield, with pro-Grey and pro-Nordic films slogging it out at the box office.

MOST CONVINCING EVIDENCE

As part of the publicity launch for a proposed venture where visitors to a theme park would have a chance to view a replica alien corpse, a former chairman of a major entertainment company appeared in a documentary that suggested that the U.S. government had an alien craft in a secret research lab (care of Roswell, naturally), that this had been covered up, and that soon we would all be meeting the aliens face to face. The chairman and his corporation must have been fairly certain of the accuracy of their information to go on record with these startling claims.

MOST MYSTERIOUS FACT

At a private preview screening of *E.T.* in the White House, President Ronald Reagan is reputed to have turned to Steven Spielberg and said: "Only three people in this entire room know how true to life this film is."

SKEPTICALLY SPEAKING

Dr. Seth Shostak of SETI, the group searching for evidence of alien civilizations in the universe, was so irritated by the major entertainment corporation's allegedly unscientific and one-sided announcement of the "truth" in the promo video for a proposed venture, that he personally complained to the chairman of the company about how the corporation was misleading children. The cynical observer might also point out that as long as the public flocks to sci-fi films and alien exhibits, profit-based organizations are going to do their very best to exploit them.

(opposite page) Dr. Seth Shostak of SETI

4 UFOs Over Iraq

On December 16, 1998, tracer fire lit up the skies of Baghdad. The ongoing "tepid war" against Saddam Hussein, which had continued since the first Gulf War had failed to remove him from power in 1991, had erupted into one of its periodic phases. The Allied air strike on Iraq's capital city was part of Operation Desert Fox and, just like the first Gulf War, it was being shown live to millions of television viewers around the world, thanks to CNN. However, that night CNN managed to capture more than the breaking news regarding Desert Fox; they also filmed a UFO hovering above Baghdad. Their footage even showed it moving away to avoid being hit by a stream of antiaircraft fire.

At the time celebrated among the UFO community as a new piece of strong evidence to prove the existence of UFOs, the incident has taken on a much wider significance among

According to some reports, U.S. pilots engaged in more battles with mysterious lights than Iraqi fighters.

certain conspiracy theorists. More and more have come to believe that there is a solid connection between UFOs seen over Iraq and America's decision to launch an invasion of Iraq in 2003. The constant patrolling and bombing of Iraqi installations by the U.K. and U.S. air forces in the northern Iraq "No-Fly Zone" produced a wealth of UFO sightings by fighter pilots and a vast number of unexplained radar contacts, with craft moving much faster than any known terrestrial fight craft. It has even been reported that Allied forces engaged in combat with a UFO in the first Gulf War thinking it was an Iraqi fighter jet. Reports also emerged that U.S. aircraft had brought down a craft of unknown origin in Saudi Arabia in 1998. Residents in the area of the crash site—officially claimed to be that of a jet fighter—were ordered to leave the area while American military engineers recovered all the wreckage for further study. However, residents claim that before they were forced to leave, they were able to establish that the craft was round and did not have any engine or wings. They also reported that even large bits of the wreckage were as light as a feather.

These intriguing tales took an unexpected twist when Russian intelligence sources suggested that a UFO had crashed in Iraq and that Hussein was engaged in a program to try and reverse engineer alien technology. At first dismissed as entirely fanciful, a number of intriguing stories relating to this claim started to surface. Among them were reports that Hussein had given sanctuary to the craft's occupants, housing them at his most secure palace, the citadel of Qalaat-e-Julundi. After the revolution that brought Hussein to power, the old royal family stronghold of Qalaat-e-Julundi became a palace for the new dictator. A vast underground bunker network was built under the existing building, already considered the most

(opposite page) Were weapons of mass destruction the only things that U.S. forces in Iraq were searching for?

impenetrable place in Iraq, as it stands on a hill surrounded by vertical precipices on three sides, plunging down to the Little Zab River. Soon after Hussein was alleged to have installed his guests there, people living in the Little Zab River Valley began to report strange lights in the sky, "dancing ghosts" seen only at night, and a number of strange deaths.

Some of those struggling to believe in any of the official reasons put forward for the second Gulf War believe that the weapons of mass destruction argument was purely a cover story created to give a pretext to an invasion of Iraq. They consider that the real reason for the vast military campaign was to prevent Hussein from reverse-engineering the crashed alien spacecraft and developing a technological advantage over the U.S. military just as the Americans had done over the Soviets with the Roswell crash in 1947.

THE STRANGE PART

After U.S. forces rolled into Baghdad, a G.I. with the 3rd Brigade, 101st Airborne Division—who was fighting in the Little Zab Valley—photographed an oblong-shaped UFO. Locals who saw the UFO close to the holy city of Najaf believed that it "had come from Allah's Gardens of Bliss to protect the Tomb of Ali." The mosque at Najaf stands over the grave of Ali, son-in-law of the prophet Muhammad. During the war, it miraculously escaped damage from the 101st Airborne's howitzer barrage, and heavy Allied bombing raids on the area around the Little Zab River Valley focused on the citadel of Qalaat-e-Julundi.

THE USUAL SUSPECTS

MJ-12

The group thought to be behind the cover-up and subsequent reverse engineering of the UFO crash at Roswell are alleged to secretly control the Joint Chiefs of Staff. They may also have close links with the Bush family through George H. W. Bush, going back to when he was director of the CIA. Having used the knowledge to ensure American supremacy since 1947, the prospect of being usurped by Saddam Hussein was unacceptable, and they were forced to create a pretext for an invasion of Iraq so they could seize the crashed craft for themselves.

Reptilian Aliens

Reptilian beings from the Draco system are often accused of having entered into a secret alliance with parts of the world's ruling elite. Rumored to be at war with the oft-sighted Greys, the Draconians may have instructed their allies in America's military and government to recover the Grey aliens being given shelter by Hussein. This was done under cover of war, rather than having to reveal themselves by a dramatic show of Draconian power in Iraq.

THE UNUSUAL SUSPECTS

The French Government

The French and Iraqi regimes enjoyed good relations, and Hussein may have been negotiating with his friends in Paris to share UFO technology with them if they could prevent him from being removed from power by George W. Bush. This would have allowed the French to lead a European challenge for global power. Right up until the moment of war, the French provided solid support for Iraq, and U.S. secretary of state Colin Powell answered "yes," when asked if France would be punished for its actions.

MOST CONVINCING EVIDENCE

Bush's claims that there was "No doubt that the Iraq regime continues to possess and conceal some of the most lethal weapons ever devised and that it threatens all mankind" were dubious, even before the post-war $500 million search of Iraq failed to find them. Though almost all of the Bush administration's claims about Iraq weapons were disproved by UN inspectors, America still went to war, which suggests there must have been an ulterior motive for the military action.

MOST MYSTERIOUS FACT

Zecharia Sitchin, one of the few people in the world able to translate ancient Sumerian cuneiform, believes that ancient texts tell how the civilization of Sumeria (based in the area occupied by modern-day Iraq) was aided by an advanced race of beings. Called the Anunnaki (Sumerian for "those who came from Heaven to Earth"), their existence would mean that Saddam is not the first ruler in that area to have been helped by extraterrestrials.

SKEPTICALLY SPEAKING

Expanding the power of America to ensure it controls the twenty-first century. The backfiring of Hussein's bluff that he had lethal weapons. A war fought on behalf of American oil companies. George W. Bush trying to prove to his father that he could kick Iraqi butt better than George H. W. could. Whatever the real explanation for the second Gulf War, surely crashed UFOs has got to be the least likely?

5 MEN IN BLACK

I f you see a UFO and report it the police, you can expect many things: ridicule, questions concerning your alcohol consumption, odd looks from friends, and perhaps a call from the local newspaper looking for a bit of light news for the next day's edition. But even worse than the preceding events, you may receive a visit from the dreaded Men in Black.

The Men in Black have long been associated with UFO sightings and phenomena. They are reported to appear at the homes of some UFO witnesses shortly after they've reported their sighting to the police or media, threatening them to keep quiet. Any materials found relating to a UFO sighting are promptly confiscated. In some cases, they have even knocked on the doors of witnesses before they've told anyone else of what they have seen, seemingly knowing everything that has happened before the witnesses had a chance to sort it all out in their heads themselves. The Men in

Hollywood's Men in Black. Part of an insidious propaganda program?

Black deliver their message in a variety of ways, from direct threats to roundabout hints, but their message always carries the same dark undertone: "Keep your mouth shut, or you'll regret it . . ."

The Men in Black are so called because of their sartorial color of choice—black. Black suits, black hats and black sunglasses . . . this intimidating color scheme extends to their cars—vintage models of Buicks, Cadillacs, or Lincolns. They have been described as having complexions ranging from olive to grey to dark, with slightly slanted eyes, speaking in an almost computer-like monotone. Their age is difficult to determine, since all of them seem to be verging towards middle-aged. They move in a robot-like manner and are perhaps best summed up in one word: "odd."

Despite their numerous appearances and incredible powers of intimidation, finding conclusive proof of the existence of the Men in Black is as slippery a task as acquiring evidence of the existence of the very UFOs they seek to protect.

THE STRANGE PART

The Men in Black definitely seem to be not of this world. Examples of this can be found in reports of MIB disintegrating coins in their hands and inexplicably trying to sing to birds in trees. In one incident, a MIB sat down on a chair, which caused his trouser leg to rise up. There, apparently grafted to his leg, was a large green wire. In other cases, MIBs are seen crossing muddy fields, yet arrive without a single spot of mud on them. In the most vicious cold weather, they will show up wearing nothing but a thin coat, oblivious to the deadly chill.

THE USUAL SUSPECTS

Aliens

In an effort to keep their activities on Earth quiet, aliens would employ the Men in Black to suppress any media attention to their activities by intimidating eyewitnesses of UFOs into fearful silence. From their inhuman way of moving and mechanical way of speaking, the MIB could be androids, programmed by the aliens involved in the sighting they are sent to suppress. Some people think that the Men in Black are aliens themselves, possibly Greys or another race, the Horlocks (a reptilian race without souls). This would explain their remarkable strangeness around other human beings.

The U.S. Government

Working in conjunction with the aliens, the U.S. government would utilize the MIB and their attendant oddities to suppress reports of UFOs. The Men in Black would be actors instructed to be as odd and bizarre as possible, thus adding to the already confused and emotional state of eyewitnesses. The MIB would be untraceable agents, not linked to any known governmental institution, thus allowing the "Powers That Be" to keep their hands clean of any violation of human rights.

THE UNUSUAL SUSPECTS

The Planet Sirius

The symbol of the Eye of Horus has been linked with secret societies in allegiance with the planet Sirius. This same symbol has been seen on some MIB, and some MIB have said they work for an organization called the Nation of the Third Eye.

The ancient Egyptian symbol of the Eye of Horus has been seen worn by the MIB.

The role they play in the plans of the denizens of Sirius is unclear.

UFO Eyewitnesses

If UFO sightings are nothing more than a complete mental breakdown of the witness involved, then the appearance of the MIB could be just a continuation of the hallucination, perhaps representing the witnesses' need for punishment and correction.

MOST CONVINCING EVIDENCE

The power of the Men in Black cannot be discounted. They have been responsible for the cancellation of *Space Review*, a magazine dedicated to studying flying saucers, and have even gone as far as gassing an eyewitness during a terrifying interrogation. It is possible that incontrovertible proof of alien existence does exist, whether it is photos, videos, or actual aliens, but it has been suppressed by the ruthless efficiency of the MIB. Research has discovered that the lineage of the Men in Black may go back as far as the Elizabethan age.

MOST MYSTERIOUS FACT

The vintage automobiles of the MIB are often illuminated from within by otherworldly greenish glows, and their clothing has a shiny alien texture to it that doesn't correspond to any known fabric on Earth.

SKEPTICALLY SPEAKING

If they were truly aliens, with the technology capable of enabling themselves to travel between the stars and capable of wiping out the memories of abductees, then why would they waste their time sending loonies in bad suits to knock on doors? Surely a good death ray would do the trick?

6 SECRET BASES ON THE MOON

The moon has always held a fascination for humanity, both as a source of romantic inspiration for poets and as an astronomical curiosity for scientists. However, is it also a secret base for the Third Reich? Apparently so.

As early as 1942, the rumors go, the Nazis landed on the moon with the aid of giant rocket saucers. These Nazi flying saucers are reported to have stood 150 feet (46 meters) high, have contained ten stories of crew compartments, and had a diameter of 180 feet (55 meters). Upon landing on the moon, the Nazis quickly began building underground bases, solidifying their hold on the lunar surface while losing their grip on power in Europe below.

This colonization continued through the 1940s, with the Nazis ferrying up more people, raw materials, and robots in their giant interplanetary Nazi saucers. After the end of the Second World War, in 1945, the Germans continued their space efforts from their Neu Schwabenland base in Earth's south polar region. This colonization continues to this day, with the full knowledge and assistance of other world powers.

There are certainly convincing photographs, taken during the Second World War, showing Nazi-produced flying craft that look remarkably similar to the classic concept of a flying saucer. These craft—going under such fabulous names as the *Vril Odin 7* and *Haunebu II*—were developed at secret bases similar to the famous rocket base Peenemunde. It is well known that German scientists, many of whom ended up as founding members of NASA after the war, had planned to turn Peenemunde into a space port and springboard for moon colonization after what they thought would be inevitable Nazi victory against the Allies.

THE STRANGE PART

Where to begin? Two things give this rumor a degree of credence. The first is the growing weight of scientific evidence that the moon is not totally arid and that the frozen ice on it could be utilized by any colony. Second, video footage taken from a NASA space shuttle clearly shows an unidentified object leaving the surface of the moon. While there may be a non-conspiratorial explanation, strange lights, inexplicable markings on the surface, and even potential structures observed by astronomers on the lunar surface push the number of odd questions needing answers to a disconcerting level.

THE USUAL SUSPECTS

The Nazi Party of Germany

Perhaps sensing the inevitability of defeat by the Allies as early as 1940, the Nazis decided to move their base of operations to a lunar plane, thus ensuring the long-term success of the Third Reich. Knowing Adolf Hitler's love of the supernatural and the fantastic, this does not seem implausible, just typically far-fetched.

The Axis Powers of Japan and Italy

Germany kept close ties with its allies during the Second World War, sharing its advances in weaponry with Italy and Japan. Rocket designs of German origin were routinely tested in Italy's research facilities, and in July 1945, at the end of the war, a German U-boat reportedly delivered a new invention to Japanese research and development units: a spherical, wingless flying machine. Working under German instructions, the Japanese constructed the device, without knowing how it worked. Once activated, it roared off into the sky in a burst of flame, never to be seen again. Shaken, the Japanese scientists decided to forget about the whole thing. However, in January 1946, a Japanese-German team, numbering in the hundreds, flew to the moon in another saucer, surviving a near crash landing.

(opposite page) A V2 rocket at the Peenemunde. Did the Nazis develop craft advanced enough to travel to the moon?

German V2 Rocket at Peenemunde, 1944

THE UNUSUAL SUSPECTS

NASA

NASA may be lying about the moon's atmosphere in order to keep other countries from wanting to explore it as well, thus ensuring a monopoly on the moon. The story goes that when the United States and Russia constructed their own moon bases in the 1950s, they were the guests of the Nazis when they landed.

Vril Society

A major mystical secret order that was the source of much of the perverse ideology behind the early philosophies of the Nazi Party, the Vril Society claimed high-ranking members of Hitler's regime, major industrialists, and powerful occultists among its ranks. It lent its name and money to the development of the mysterious *Vril* flying craft. It is known that some members believed the Aryan race developed from aliens who landed in Sumeria around 4500 BCE and were viewed as gods. Could Vril have been the power behind the establishment of Nazi moon bases?

Aliens

Some conspiriologists believe that the Nazis were in league with extraterrestrials and that the many advances they made in genetics and rocket science can be traced to a helping hand from beyond the stars. Debate rages over exactly which type of alien was assisting Hitler, but the favorites are the Aryan-looking Nordics rather than the Greys. However, given the type of experimentation on humans the Greys seem to love, and the depraved medical research performed by some of the human monsters of the Nazi regime, no one is ruling out an alliance with that particular branch of villainous space scum.

MOST CONVINCING EVIDENCE

The only proof of the American landing on the moon comes from photographs published by NASA. However, over recent years, these photos have been classed as fake because they are full of inconsistencies. Shadow lengths are at odds with the sun, the directions of shadows vary within pictures, and there is plenty of evidence of the photos having been taken with the use of large sources of artificial light. If the photographs from NASA are not to be trusted, what else should we doubt?

MOST MYSTERIOUS FACT

There have not been any lunar landings—at least in the public's eyes—in over thirty years. Is this to distract the world's attentions from the colonies—Nazi, Russian, and American, with populations estimated at over 40,000—at work there?

SKEPTICALLY SPEAKING

The drives needed to power such huge saucers—listed by conspiracy theorists as "free energy tachyon drives"—cannot help but raise eyebrows. But with the reverse engineering associated with the salvaged technology from the Roswell crash and the lack of photos of the moon's dark side, one can't help but wonder.

7 THE RENDLESHAM LANDING—ENGLAND'S ROSWELL

There are mean-spirited cynics who will tell you that conspiracy theorists live only for the moment when they can rub their hands together and say, "I told you so." But in the annals of alien conspiracies, there is only one case where the conspiracy research can leap up like an overactive dog and shout, "I told you so, it is official—there was a conspiracy!" That case is Rendlesham.

On December 27, 1980, an unidentified flying object landed in a clearing in Rendlesham Forest next to the joint USAF air bases of Bentwaters and Woodbridge, near Ipswich, England. Deputy Base Commander Lieutenant Colonel Charles Halt and several of his men witnessed the landing. It was tracked by British military radar and left behind physical evidence. Twelve years later, a British parliamentary watchdog ruled that the U.K. government had attempted to cover up all of the above facts. In 2002, parliamentary ombudsman Ann Abraham ruled that the U.K.

A UFO sighting linked to U.S. nuclear bombers? No wonder it is a conspiracy.

Ministry of Defense had refused to divulge full details of the Rendlesham witness accounts and conspired to prevent knowledge of the event from ever becoming known.

The incident is regarded as one of the most important UFO sightings ever and has become known as the "English Roswell." Possibly, it is just coincidence that both cases involve the U.S. military and happened close to highly sensitive military bases with links to top-secret arms of American nuclear defense structure. Alongside being the only alien conspiracy where a government attempt to cover up the facts has been proven and exposed, no other case has as many staggering eyewitness accounts by highly credible military professionals.

Shortly after midnight on the day after Christmas, radar screens at RAF Watton in Norfolk showed the sudden appearance of an object near Rendlesham Forest. Given that the twin airbases leased to the USAF on the perimeter of the forest housed a vast stockpile of weapons, alarm intensified when the object suddenly disappeared before reappearing without warning on the radar of the Bentwaters base. While further radar confirmations of the strange craft were coming in from other tracking stations, three military policemen saw light in the trees outside the back gate of the airfield and set off, fearing a crash. In his report of that night, Deputy Base Commander Lt. Col. Halt wrote, "They reported seeing a strange glowing object in the forest. Metallic in appearance and triangular in shape approximately two to three meters [six to nine feet] across the base and two meters [six feet] high. It illuminated the entire forest with a white light. The object itself has a pulsating red light on top and a bank of blue lights underneath. The object was hovering or on legs. As the patrolmen approached it maneuvered through the trees and disappeared. At this time animals on a nearby farm went into a frenzy."

The next night, Lt. Col. Halt joined a patrol that found three depressions on the forest floor where the object had been sighted. Radiation readings of ten times the normal level were discovered, and as they were investigating, the craft returned.

Several years after the incident, Halt released an eighteen-minute audiocassette made on the night of the encounter. It makes chilling listening, especially the moment when another officer on the patrol sees the craft and shouts, "Look at the colors! [expletive]!" The tape also records the panic-stricken men as they see a beam from the craft disabling electrical devices in the area for a time and other military personnel in the area recording the event with both still and video cameras.

Given the impeccable witnesses and multiple types of physical evidence, you might think the public would at last be told that things that were unidentifiable and flew really did exist. However, in the years that followed, both the American and British militaries did everything in their power to cover up the Rendlesham Forest incident. It even seemed as if other shadowy elements were also involved in a conspiracy to enforce silence, discrediting, scaring, and threatening any-one witnessing the case or who had knowledge of it. In 1983, conspiracy researchers got their first major break when a copy of a memo written by Lt. Col. Halt to the British Ministry of Defense was released under the Freedom of Information Act. With the first part of the puzzle out in the open, the battle to reveal the truth really began.

THE STRANGE PART

As more and more of the U.S. military witnesses to the landing on the second night were identified, one USAF security patrolman, Larry Warren, even went public with an account claiming that he saw three "aeronaut entities" communicating with senior officers. The next morning, he and colleagues were checked for radiation exposure and instructed to sign statements, which merely mentioned seeing "unusual lights." The statements were arranged by members of the National Security Agency and warned them not to discuss what they had seen.

THE USUAL SUSPECTS

The NSA

The U.S. National Security Agency had a strong presence at the bases and played a key role in attempting to keep the landing secret. The NSA has an alleged contact and humans-for-advanced-technology exchange program with the Greys, and Rendlesham was purely a routine business meeting that was accidentally witnessed by Lt. Col. Halt and his men.

Project Phoenix

Project Phoenix is an ultrasecret program run by America's Defense Advanced Research Projects Agency. One element of Project Phoenix may be dealing with advanced microwave, laser, and hologram weapons meant to create totally convincing illusions to baffle and demoralize the enemy. Rendlesham may have been an experiment to test the credulity of crack troops as well as assessing the impact on morale among elite warriors of these weapons.

THE UNUSUAL SUSPECTS

Parallel Earth Travelers

In medieval times, in an area close to Rendlesham, two mysterious green-skinned children were found, causing some to speculate that this part of Suffolk is home to a gateway to a parallel Earth. The visitors to Rendlesham may not have been extraterrestrial visitors but instead, extradimensional. Either they took a wrong turn or were on a scouting mission to our Earth.

Zeta Reticulans

Grey humanoid aliens from Zeta Reticuli were scouting the U.S. bases, as elements of the American military are in a secret alliance with reptilian aliens from the Sirius system. Their craft got into trouble and they were forced to land to make repairs behind enemy lines. However, luckily for the Zeta Reticulans, the soldiers at Rendlesham did not know they were at war and therefore let the space reptiles' sworn enemies slip away.

MOST CONVINCING EVIDENCE

Despite the fact that it was tracked by radar, and left impressions in the ground and massive radiation readings, the military and others later tried to claim that the event was the revolving beam of the Orford Ness lighthouse, five miles away. The depressions in the earth were merely rabbit diggings, and the radiation was at natural levels. Many witnesses were sacked, defamed, harassed, stalked, and threatened by the authorities as well as military intelligence agents and shadowy Men in Black—all of which is a bit over the top if the soldiers and civilians had just mistaken a lighthouse!

MOST MYSTERIOUS FACT

Author and society gossip columnist Georgina Bruni became a conspiracy researcher on the subject of Rendlesham and wrote a classic book on the case. At a social event in 1997, she seized her chance to ask former British prime minister Margaret Thatcher about the landing. Thatcher was annoyed at being questioned about Rendlesham and railed at Bruni, "You can't tell the people."

SKEPTICALLY SPEAKING

Is anyone surprised that the U.K. government and the U.S. military conspired to keep quiet about something strange landing close to an air force base housing enough nuclear weapons to turn all of Europe into a radioactive wasteland?

8 ROSWELL

It was July 3, 1947, when W. W. "Mac" Brazel saddled his horse and rode out to check his sheep on his sprawling New Mexico ranch. There had been a thunderstorm the night before, and Brazel felt concerned for his animals' safety. But as he rode, he came across bits of strange wreckage strewn across the land. He also discovered what appeared to be a wreck of some sort. A huge gouge had been dug into the earth, running for hundreds of feet. Mystified, Brazel retrieved a piece of the strange material that littered the ground and showed it to a neighbor. Wondering if he was holding something from a government project or possibly a UFO, he drove into nearby Roswell to tell his story to the local sheriff, George Wilcox, and by doing so, launched one of the most enduring nesting grounds for conspiracies in the twentieth century.

Modern-day inhabitants of Roswell have turned their town into a tourist spot.

The truth about the incident at Roswell has remained hidden behind government subterfuge and the unreliability of aging eyewitnesses. What is undisputed is that Wilcox dutifully reported the wreckage to intelligence officer Major Jesse Marcel of the 509th Bomb Squad. For the next few days, the site was closed off as the U.S. Air Force removed the wreckage. On July 8, 1947, a press release prepared by the USAF reported the debris was from a "flying disc." The following day, however, the government quickly retracted the story, stating firmly that the mysterious debris was not from a flying saucer, but merely the wreckage of a crashed weather balloon.

And there the story ended, or so the U.S. government hoped. But strange stories began to grow, gaining strength by the unusual silence from military and government leaders. Among these stories were tales that it was indeed a crashed flying saucer and that the government was covering it up; that there were actual alien bodies aboard the ship, and even that some of the aliens had survived. Sixty years have passed since the incident at Roswell. Conspiracy theories have flourished, generating much media attention and providing an eternal burr beneath the skin of the government. Eventually the U.S. Air Force released a report, The Roswell Report: Case Closed, on June 24, 1994, in a vain attempt to shut the lid on perhaps the greatest Pandora's box the conspiracy world has ever known. Not surprisingly, it failed.

THE STRANGE PART

During the cleanup of debris, Glenn Dennis, a mortician working in a Roswell funeral home, answered a few phone calls from the morgue at the local airfield. The mortuary officer there was looking for information on how to best preserve bodies that had been outside for a few days without suffering further contamination of the bodies' tissues. He also requested small, hermetically sealed coffins.

THE USUAL SUSPECTS

The U.S. Government

A crashed UFO would have been a major technological windfall for the U.S. government, and it would have wanted to keep such a find as secret as possible. Some people feel that the Roswell crash led the military into trying to decipher the mystery of the downed craft, reverse-engineering the alien technology to derive new weapons and antigravity capabilities. President Harry Truman allegedly visited the crash site and may even have spoken to surviving aliens. Shortly afterwards, Truman instigated the removal of all of the UFO crash material, including that found at Roswell, into the keeping of an anonymous multinational syndicate that now controls all UFO technology.

The U.S. government has even been accused of torturing the alien survivors of Roswell, if not killing them outright, according to a secret policy of dealing with extraterrestrials.

Other, less fantastic theories place the blame on the military, testing secret planes built using Albert Einstein's withdrawn work on gravity field theory.

The Greys

There's no shortage of theories that state the Greys are using mankind to perfect genetic manipulations in order to save their own race. Alarmed that mankind had graduated to using nuclear weapons in 1945 (in much the same way we would have been if we discovered a pet hamster with an Uzi), the Greys reportedly began reconnaissance missions around military bases. This could have been the case at Roswell, where two ships may have collided, or the reconnaissance craft could simply have been struck by lightning.

THE UNUSUAL SUSPECTS

The Soviets

During the raging Cold War paranoia, it was suspected that the Soviets might have perfected their offensive missile capability with pilfered Nazi technology. The Roswell debris could have been the remains of a failed missile attack.

(opposite page) U.S. president Harry Truman

Hollow Earth Mole Men

There is a theory that the middle of Earth is a hollow space containing land masses, a sun and oceans. According to that theory, the race living there might have been alarmed, much like the Greys, at the rise of nuclear testing by the creatures living on the surface of the planet. Flying out of the huge polar holes that lead to the hollow part of Earth, these "Mole Men" may have crashed their ship on a reconnaissance mission.

MOST CONVINCING EVIDENCE

The need for the air force to release a "final report" implies a guilty conscience. If there was really nothing to Roswell, why go to the trouble, expense, and possible ridicule of commissioning and publishing a report? The sudden leap forward in technology that followed the Roswell crash, especially the invention of transistors, is suspicious.

MOST MYSTERIOUS FACT

After driving out to the airfield hospital, the Roswell mortician, Glenn Dennis, saw several bits of wreckage carved with strange engravings. Speaking to a nurse there, she explained about the bodies, going so far as to draw him pictures on a prescription pad. A few days later, she was

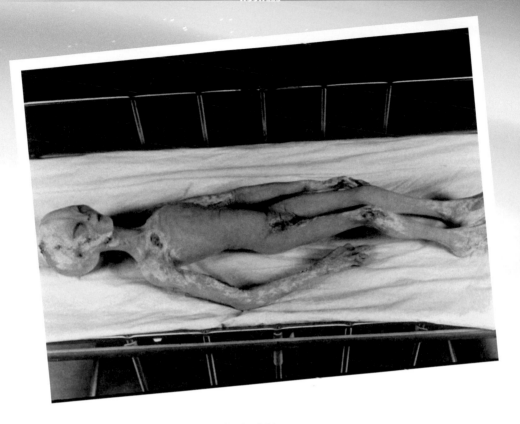

Is this what the Roswell "aliens" looked like?

mysteriously assigned to a post in England and then seemed, apparently, to drop off the face of the earth.

SKEPTICALLY SPEAKING

The wild variations in the accounts of several "eyewitnesses" and the pure schlock of such gems as the purported Roswell alien autopsy video give this potentially devastating event all the appeal of a circus sideshow. It has become the alien conspiracy equivalent of Elvis sightings.

9 SPACE SABOTAGE

Traveling to the stars has always been a daunting task, but is it being made more difficult than it need be? Is someone—or something—doing its best to keep humankind on Earth by sabotaging space flight after space flight? The problem has become so widespread that NASA has jokingly referred to this enigmatic and often deadly force as the "Great Galactic Ghoul." But is it the subject for levity, or something far more terrifying?

The high incidence rate of spaceflight accidents, disappearances, and technological foul-ups would have crippled any other endeavor that didn't have the benefit of government funding. From simple faults such as wires burning out in satellite systems to the tragedy of the *Challenger* explosion, the Great Galactic Ghoul shows no national preference; both Russian and American space programs have been plagued by its disruptive hand.

Recent examples include the fiasco surrounding the Hubble telescope. Once in space, the much-vaunted telescope was found to be far from perfect, thus making its pictures far more blurred than expected. An expensive repair mission was needed, but the Hubble pictures are still being discounted as more a triumph of selective filters, designed to hide the telescope's imperfections, than the groundbreaking shots the project's supporters claim them to be.

Another example was the Mars *Explorer* mission of 1993, which was launched to take closer pictures of the mysterious Cydonia region of Mars. Just as the craft was entering Martian orbit, it suddenly stopped functioning. Other failures include the Soviet *Koralb 11* (blew up) and *Sputnik 24* (blew up); NASA's *Mariner 3* (missed Mars), *Mariner 8* (fell into Atlantic), and *Apollo 13* missions; and the fiery deaths of the astronauts in the space shuttle. The list goes on and on, and it is either a testament to staggering incompetence or evidence of an ongoing act of sabotage, perhaps even on a galactic scale.

THE STRANGE PART

Missions to Mars fare the worst when it comes to sabotage. One of the most disturbing was the fate of the Russian Phobos probes. Launched in 1988, the two probes were sent to investigate Phobos, the smaller of Mars's two moons. The Russians were interested in the irregular orbital patterns, which led many to believe Phobos was either an artificial

A high number of expensive space exploration launches end in a disastrous manner.

construction or perhaps hollow. The first probe was somehow lost on the journey from Earth. *Phobos 2* made it to Mars, and on its way to the small moon took photographs of a cylindrical-shaped shadow on the surface of Phobos. Shortly after that, the probe was destroyed. Its final picture, beamed back to Russia, has been declared too sensitive to release to the public. On the night that final picture was sent, Orthodox Russian priests were asked to go to the *Phobos 2* Control Center in Moscow to discuss the pictures received.

THE USUAL SUSPECTS

NASA

As horrible as it sounds, especially with human lives being lost in some accidents, it is possible that a secret contingent within NASA could be sabotaging missions in order to satisfy elements in the U.S. government that do not want the space program to discover the alien presence surrounding Earth. Corresponding dissidents would, of course, exist in the Russian space program.

Competing Contractors

The financial windfall associated with landing a lucrative government contract would prove irresistible to many businessmen. The best way to succeed in the cutthroat tendering process would be to discredit fellow competitors, using whatever means available, including sabotage. The power of the dollar, especially one from a government source, would easily overcome the sanctity of human lives in the eyes of many.

Also suspected: the FBI; MJ-12; sheer human incompetence.

THE UNUSUAL SUSPECTS

The Greys

For reasons of their own, it would be in the best interests of the Greys to keep Earth isolated from the rest of the universe. If the Greys are rebellious slaves escaping from their masters and using human genetic material to reproduce and save themselves from the degradation of their cloned bodies, it simply would not do to have mankind drawing the attention of other alien races, particularly those masters.

Martians

The surprising number of incidents involving Mars missions goes beyond pure coincidence. The Monuments on Mars indicate that there was—or may still be—life on Mars, life that may wish to be left alone or that will make its presence known in its own good time. The breakdowns, disappearances, and erratic behavior of craft around the Red Planet have led some NASA employees to joke about a Great Galactic Ghoul living in between the asteroid belt and Mars. Perhaps this ghoul is nothing more than a disgruntled Martian.

MOST CONVINCING EVIDENCE

Before the launch of the Mars *Observer*, on September 25, 1992, NASA technicians examined its outer housing for a routine check. Inside, they were shocked to find the probe filled with garbage. This garbage included metal filings, dirt, paper, fibers, and plaster of Paris. Even though Hurricane Andrew had blown through the area, it was impossible for debris of this kind to have entered the probe driven by the force of the storm alone.

Maybe it is not so surprising that of the thirty-five attempts to reach the planet, only twelve have succeeded. Of these, nine were attempts to land on the surface, but only three survived. The rest crashed or exploded in orbit. Even the successful ones had problems. *Sojourner*, which was launched aboard the Mars *Pathfinder* in 1996, could only manage to move about 300 feet from its landing zone.

MOST MYSTERIOUS FACT

In July 1998, the *Galileo* spacecraft was passing Europa, one of Jupiter's moons, when it suddenly stopped transmitting information. It has long been speculated that Europa, along with Mars, may be able to sustain life.

SKEPTICALLY SPEAKING

We are a race that has trouble programming our DVD players. Is it any wonder our spaceships keep blowing up?

10 REVERSE ENGINEERING

Have you ever felt that the world was moving too fast? Have you ever wondered at the amazing technological leaps mankind seems to have made in such a relatively short amount of time? Have you ever felt a pang of uneasiness when you consider that humanity went from barely being able to fly a crude airplane to walking on the moon in under seventy years?

The unprecedented way humanity's level of technology increased in the twentieth century is simply baffling and may be a sign of one of the most pervasive conspiracies of all time. While the scientific community pats itself on the back and ascribes such progress to the diligence and ingenuity of its members, a look at the "innovations" of the last few decades seem to owe more to "intervention" than ingenuity.

In fact, many theorists feel that the true force behind the current technological juggernaut is not elbow grease and endless nights burning the midnight oil, but alien assistance.

For reasons unknown to the general public, governments worldwide are reverse-engineering alien technology, that is, taking apart alien artifacts to discover what makes them work, then applying that knowledge to their own ends. This knowledge is putting us light years ahead of where we should be technologically and, perhaps, even culturally. Like children playing with fire, we are not mature enough to handle it and are in serious danger of getting burned.

THE STRANGE PART

Most of the major leaps in technology occur after 1947, from more powerful computers to the Apollo lunar missions. It was in 1947, coincidentally enough, that the U.S. government allegedly salvaged a crashed UFO from Roswell, New Mexico.

THE USUAL SUSPECTS

The U.S. Government

It has long been theorized that a UFO (or UFOs) crashed near Roswell and Corona in New Mexico in 1947 and that the U.S. government quickly made off with the remains. Caught in the Cold War with the USSR, the United States was desperate for any military advantage and so began the slow process of reverse-engineering the alien technology found aboard the crashed flying saucers. Much of this reverse engineering is thought to occur at the infamous Area 51, a secret military testing site in New Mexico.

Has alien technology played a role in advancing U.S. military craft?

The Greys

In exchange for being allowed to kidnap and experiment on humans with impunity, one theory has the U.S. government—and possibly other governments—agreeing to look the other way in exchange for alien technology. This would explain why incidents of abduction and UFO sightings are treated with ridicule by government authorities as they try to divert attention from what is truly going on—the sale of humanity for capital gain.

THE UNUSUAL SUSPECTS

Time Travelers

Time travelers could be bringing technology in the hope that leaving their futuristic gadgetry with us could change circumstances in their time, altering it to their advantage. Other theories state that the U.S. government has experimented with short-range time travel and is bringing back technology from our own future. Similar theories lay the blame on dimensional travel, with advanced technology coming from more advanced versions of our own present day.

Benevolent Aliens

In preparation for an invasion force coming to Earth, benevolent aliens have provided world powers with the technology to defend themselves, as evidenced in the Star Wars satellites. The advances seen by the everyday populace—cell phones, microwaves, home computers—are merely lucrative spin-offs generated by reverse-engineering of this technology and are a bonus for the government contractors that undertake secret defense work.

MOST CONVINCING EVIDENCE

Perhaps the most incriminating bit of technology that ushered in the current wave of progress was the transistor. This has been rumored to be a direct result of reverse-engineering work on the crashed ship at Roswell. Other more sinister applications of this alien science could be the U.S. military's weaponry, including the B-2 stealth bomber.

MOST MYSTERIOUS FACT

Curious citizens who have reported seeing strange lights that resemble UFOs around Area 51, and an NBC News crew that filmed something odd in the sky in 1992, have had to contend with armed forces harassing them and confiscating cameras and video equipment. Some people have even been chased by black helicopters, which are often seen around areas of suspected alien activity.

SKEPTICALLY SPEAKING

One problem with the reverse-engineering theory is that it assumes humans are brilliant. If we went back in time and handed Mr. Cro-Magnon a Pentium laptop, a remote-control garage-door opener, and a ThighMaster, the reverse-engineering theory would have us believe that he'd be founding MagnonSoft in ten years. Sadly, he'd probably grunt at the items and then drop them on to someone's head. Well, maybe he'd keep the ThighMaster.

Glossary

abduction The carrying away of a person, usually for unlawful purposes.

androids Robots in human form.

annals Chronicles or records, usually arranged in a yearly sequence.

benevolent Characterized by doing good deeds.

carrion Dead and rotting flesh.

cauterize To burn or sear tissue, usually with a hot iron tool.

conspiriologist One involved in studying conspiracies or cover-ups.

credence Believability.

decipher To decode.

disinformation False information spread to obscure the truth.

eviscerating To disembowel; take out the entrails.

exsanguination Removing or draining blood.

extrapolation Predicting trends based on past behavior or known information.

forensic Related to the application of scientific knowledge in solving legal problems.

grisly Inspiring horror or intense fear.

hallucination Perception, typically a sight or sound, with no reality.

hermetically sealed Airtight.

hologram A three-dimensional image created from a laser.

impeccable Flawless; free from fault or blame.

incontrovertible Not open to question.

inscrutable Not easily interpreted or understood.

occultist One who believes in or studies the influence of the supernatural.

pilfered Stolen.

premillennial Related to period immediately before the turn of a millennium or, sometimes, the turn of a century.

profane Impure or unholy.

propaganda The spreading of information or disinformation for the purpose of helping or hindering a specific cause.

sadistic Cruel; taking pleasure in someone else's pain.

sartorial Related to clothing.

schlock Of low quality or value.

sci-fi Abbreviation of "science fiction."

subterfuge Deception used to conceal or otherwise help in evasion.

telepathic Communicated directly from one mind to another.

tracer Ammunition containing a chemical that lights up, creating a trail that aids in aiming at the target.

tractor beam Hypothetical device able to draw in objects.

ultrasonic Operating at vibrations higher than the human ear can hear.

virulent Severely poisonous or harmful.

For More Information

International UFO Museum and Research Center
114 North Main Street
Roswell, NM 88201
(505) 625-9495
Web site: http://www.iufomrc.com

The J. Allen Hynek Center for UFO Studies (CUFOS)
2457 W. Peterson
Chicago, IL 60659
(773) 271-3611
Web site: http://www.cufos.org

National Aeronautics and Space Administration (NASA)
   Headquarters
Suite 1M32
Washington, DC 20546-0001
(202) 358-0001
Web site: http://www.nasa.gov

NEWTON COUNTY PUBLIC LIBRARY
ROSELAWN BRANCH

National UFO Reporting Center
P. O. Box 700
Davenport, WA 99122
(206) 722-3000
Web site: http://www.nuforc.org

WEB SITES

Due to the changing nature of Internet links, Rosen Publishing has developed an online list of Web sites related to the subject of this book. This site is updated regularly. Please use this link to access the list:

http://www.rosenlinks.com/mc/unem

For Further Reading

Berlitz, Charles, and William Moore. *The Roswell Incident.*
New York, NY: Berkley Books, 1990.

Birnes, William J. *The UFO Encyclopedia.* New York, NY:
Pocket Books, 2004.

Corrales, Scott. Chupacabras: *And Other Mysteries.*
Murfreesboro, TN: Greenleaf, 1997.

Keith, Jim. *Casebook on the Men in Black.* Lilburn, GA:
IllumiNet Press, 1997.

Marrs, Jim. Alien *Agenda: Investigating the Extraterrestrial
Presence Among Us.* New York: NY: HarperCollins, 1997.

O'Brien, Christopher. *Enter the Valley: UFOs, Religious
Miracles, Cattle Mutilations, and Other Unexplained
Phenomena in the San Luis Valley.* New York, NY: St.
Martin's Press, 1999.

Randle, Kevin D. *The Roswell Encyclopedia.* New York, NY:
HarperCollins, 2000.

Redfern, Nick. *On the Trail of the Saucer Spies: UFOs and
Government Surveillance.* San Antonio, TX: Anomalist
Books, 2006.

Sparks, Jim. *The Keepers: An Alien Message for the Human
Race.* Orem, UT: Granite Publishing, 2006.

Spielberg, Steven. *Close Encounters of the Third Kind.* New
York, NY: Delacorte Press, 1977.

Strieber, Whitley. *Communion.* New York, NY: Random
House, 1990.

INDEX

PHOTO CREDITS

Cover, p. 7 Darren Winter/Corbis; p. 14 Phil Shermeister/Corbis; p. 20 Collection Cinéma/Photos12.com; p. 24 Seth Shostak/SETI; pp. 38, 55 Mark Peterson/Corbis; pp. 43, 61 Topham; p. 58 Library of Congress; p. 64 © NASA.

Designer: Tom Forget; **Editor:** Christopher Roberts

001.9   89238
SOUTHWE   Southwell, David,
             Unsolved
             extraterrestrial
             mysteries
                14.95

89238

R

NEWTON COUNTY PUBLIC LIBRARY
ROSELAWN BRANCH

CO, INC. 38-3011